Buying Your First Home
A Guide for the Complete Process

GRETA NELSON

ISBN: 684775
ISBN-13: 978-1542729772

DEDICATION

Dedicated to Home Buyers Everywhere

CONTENTS

ACKNOWLEDGMENTS

Michael Nelson, for support
Tim Davis, for inspiration

To Rent or

To Buy-

That Is the Question!

1 TO RENT OR TO BUY?

There are advantages and disadvantages to both renting or owning your home, depending on your needs, at this time. Here are several considerations for you to review:

Down Payment

An equivalent expense in renting is the initial deposit, equal to the first and last month's rent. All or a portion of this may be returned to you at the end of your lease. Any damages caused while renting can cause you to forfeit part or all of your deposit. What you see as decorating may be interpreted as damage by your landlord.

As a general rule, the down payment on a home is 20% of the purchase price. For a home priced at $250,000, that is a down payment of $50,000. For a large number of people that is a large amount of money to pay out at one time. Do not be discouraged, as there are several lending options that are available to pay less than 20% as a down payment. Generally, the more money you put down, the better the lending terms.

Fixed Expenses

When renting, the landlords can change rent or utility prices at the end of each leasing period.

A fixed rate mortgage lets homeowners know exactly what their payments will be for as long as it takes to pay off their home.

Customization

While some landlords allow renters to paint, it is rare

that you will be able to do any big renovation projects, and may be interpreted as damage by the landlord, when you plan to move.

The average homeowner spends about $2300 on home improvements every year in their homes, increasing the usefulness for the owners and the resale value when sold.

Taxes

The renter does not pay any property taxes, but also has no tax deductions related to homeownership. The homeowner has property taxes to pay, rates determined by the area you buy. Taxes are usually rolled into an escrow account by your lender, so you pay ahead into an account for taxes to be paid retrospectively each year. Those taxes provide a deduction on your itemized annual income taxes.

Maintenance

Renters typically aren't responsible for fixing things

when they break. However, waiting for maintenance to be done can be an issue.

When you own your home, you must be prepared for maintenance and paying for it on a regular basis.

Each year, homeowners should budget 1-2% of the purchase price of your home for ongoing maintenance costs.

Stability

When renting, a landlord can decide to stop renting to a tenant at the end of a lease, and if a landlord sells the property, tenants may have to move on short notice.

Owning a home allows a family to find a place where they know they can stay.

Insurance

The average cost of renter's insurance is $12 a month ($144 annually) to cover the cost of property worth $30,000, plus $100,000 in liability coverage.

To estimate the annual costs of insuring a home that you own, divide the cost of the home by 1000, and multiply by $3.50. For a $250,000 home, the cost of insurance would be $73 per month, or $875 per year.

Flexibility

Renters have the option of leaving a place at the end of a lease, and don't have money tied up in their homes.

A home is not only a place to stay for homeowners, but is also a financial investment. It may take weeks or months to sell a home, if you need to relocate.

Buying a home in a desirable area helps in increasing your home's value over time and its salability if you need to sell.

From purely a financial standpoint, if you are planning to own your home for 8-10 years or more it is definitely more cost efficient to buy that to rent.

But there are many reasons to buy a home, so lets

look at a blueprint of the process to get started!
NOTES:

_____

_____

_____

_____

_____

_____

_____

_____

_____

_____

_____

_____

More Than You Ever Wanted to Know About Credit Scores!

2 KNOW YOUR CREDITWORTHINESS

Before diving into your home search, check your credit report for errors. Consumers are entitled to one free credit report per year at www.annualcreditreport.com The process for fixing mistakes can be time consuming, so it's important for buyers to look at their credit history before starting their house hunt. The higher your credit score, the better your terms will be from a lender. A credit score of 620 is acceptable to most lenders, but the higher the better. So let's talk about what goes into your credit score.

Payment History- this accounts for 35% of your credit score, so paying bills on time, on a regular basis is important. This includes the type of accounts you have, payment information on credit cards, installment and mortgage loans, public record items and collection notices, and details on late or missed payments.

Outstanding Debt- this determines 30% of your credit score and can impact your debt to income ratio (more on that later) when applying for a mortgage. This includes the amount owed on different accounts, the number of different accounts, and how close you are to each credit limit.

Credit History- this accounts for 15% of your score and includes the length of your credit history, the durability of your accounts, and the frequency of use of each account.

Pursuit of New Credit- this determines 10% of your

score, looking at the number of new accounts, the duration of the new account, number of requests for new accounts, and recent credit history

Types of Credit in Use- accounts for 10% of your score and examines the number and type of different credit accounts.

Knowing these numbers ahead of time allows you to make the biggest impact in the shortest amount of time in order to increase your credit score. Since the biggest factor is "Payment History", get into the habit of paying bills on time or before they are due. Whatever system you need to set up in order to accomplish this is well worth your efforts, when the time comes to purchase your home.

Two other types of debt can negatively impact your ability to buy a home- medical bills and student loans. Medical bills that go to collection will show up under the "Payment History" section of your credit score.

Student loans may impact your debt to income ratio when determining the amount of loan you qualify for. Notes:

_____

_____

_____

_____

_____

_____

_____

_____

_____

_____

_____

_____

Isn't It Too Soon to Call A Realtor?

3 WORK WITH A REAL ESTATE PROFESSIONAL

This seems counter intuitive: Hire a Realtor before we know what we want and where we want to live and how much we can borrow?

Let me explain. Your Realtor is like the director of a play. In a play you have the actors onstage that everyone sees and applauds. You hear the musicians and the sound effects, see the costumes and the sets, see the lighting and its impact on the stage, yet you never see the people responsible for this. But the director is interacting with all of them to be sure the play comes together and is a hit!

You have the same situation when you buy a house. Your Realtor orchestrates working with a banker, lenders, title companies, real estate attorneys, inspectors, the seller, the buyer, engineers, and sometimes construction managers to complete the transaction. Some of these professionals talk to one or two of all the people required to complete the transaction. But the Realtor talks to **ALL** – just like the director of a play, and does it during their working hours, which may also be when you are at work.

Your realtor can also put you in touch with appropriate lenders to suit your situation – as we will discuss in the next chapter.

More importantly, your Realtor listens to you and your needs when buying a home. They make you aware of new construction in the area that may meet your needs.

They have information on school districts, gated

community requirements and restrictions, and market trends in each area. They can help you to find a home in an area with specific lifestyle preferences that you have and help you negotiate the best price for your home. Over 90% of buyers now search online prior to contacting a Realtor, but many of the homes they see online are already sold or off the market. Your Realtor will have the most current choices for you to review when you are ready to buy. The best part of this is that, as a buyer, you are not paying your Realtor. They get paid a portion of the listing agent's fee when the home is purchased. Realtors want to develop a long term relationship with buyers in order to work with you again and get referrals from you for other buyers. So develop a relationship with a Realtor that will work with you to meet your needs. It is what you deserve to help you find the home of your dreams.

Notes:

How Do I Know

How Much I Want to Borrow,

If I Haven't

Found A House Yet?

4 GET PRE-APPROVED FOR A MORTGAGE

This also seems counter intuitive: Get pre-approved before you have even looked at houses yet. Bear with me though, and it will make sense.

In addition to your credit scores, another factor that lenders examine is your "debt to income ratio". This number helps lenders predict your ability to manage the payments on the borrowed money and will also impact the terms of any loan you receive. Your debt to income ratio is all of your monthly debt payments divided by your gross monthly income. Your gross monthly income is the amount of money you have earned before your taxes and other deductions are taken. For example, if you pay $1500 a month for your rent, another $100 for an auto loan, and $400 a month for the rest of your debts, your monthly debt payments are $2000. If your gross monthly income is $6000, then your debt to income ratio is 33%. (2000 is 33% of 6000.) The highest debt to income ratio a borrower can have and still get a qualified mortgage is 43%.

Obtain offers from at least three mortgage lenders, before choosing one. Your Realtor can assist you by recommending professional lenders they have worked successfully with in the past.

Once you have determined the mortgage lender you want to work with, ask for a Pre-Approval Letter from the as Proof of Funds. This helps you determine your price range and avoid looking at properties that you cannot afford. It will also give you leverage in presenting an offer to sellers when you have found your perfect home, as the sellers then know you are serious about buying and have done your homework in getting yourself "ready to buy". A Pre-Approval Letter is as if you have "proof of funds" and is different than being "Prequalified to buy". Prequalified means that you have not submitted any paperwork to a lender, but they are stating that if you are telling them the truth about your credit rating, income, and debt to income ratio, they would work with you. You can see how the

"Pre-Approval Letter" holds considerably more weight for a seller and which buyer they would want to enter a contract with – this is great leverage for you!

There are many options for down payments to discuss with your mortgage lender. Most lenders recommend 20% of the purchase price. With 20% as a down payment you instantly gain equity in your home, can get a lower interest rate on your mortgage, and sellers see you as a more serious and qualified buyer.

Notes:

_____

_____

_____

_____

_____

_____

_____

_____

_____

_____

_____

Let's Go

Look at Houses!

But

Which Ones?

5 FINDING YOUR HOME

Everyone's needs, in terms of a community, vary depending on their stage in life. Couples raising a family care about schools and safety. Singles pay close attention to entertainment, nightlife and job opportunities. Recreational activities may be a deciding factor in finding a home with access to golf, tennis, boating or other hobbies. Pool and beach access is always a priority in Southwest Florida- do you want a private pool or one in your community for occasional use? If this is a home that you may later sell, you want to consider property value trends in the area. A Realtor can assist in focusing your home search in the location that suits your needs.

Some considerations to also think about include the distance of your commute to work. When there are two people employed in the household, what is a good location for both in terms of a work commute. Also, do you want a newly built home or buying in an established neighborhood. A Realtor can assist with the negotiations with both, but the realtors onsite at community development can only sell inside that development. Easy questions about number of bedrooms and bathrooms come first. Pets? – those can limit where you will be looking, as many gated communities have rules governing number and size of pets. Amenities offered in gated communities can also be an overwhelming number of options. Some communities have Homeowner Association (HOA) fees in addition to mandatory fees for recreational activities like golf, tennis, or clubs.

A newly developing area may have additional taxes to support building schools, roads and other municipal services in that area.

All of this information is available upon request and your Realtor has access to it online and can make the calls for you to help you narrow your search.

Now that you have worked with a lender to determine how much you can afford, you also want to assess now, what additional fees you can comfortably afford. As you meet with your Realtor, they can assist you with these questions, do the legwork in finding requirements in each community and help you find your dream home.

Notes:

_____

_____

_____

_____

_____

_____

_____

_____

_____

_____

_____

_____

When Can I Go Look at Houses?

6 CHOICES! CHOICES!

You and your lender have determined your price range for home buying. You and your Realtor have looked at all the variables, must haves, would like to have and can't live without options. Now what?

Now your Realtor can start scouring online choices for you and send these choices to you online. They can arrange for you to safely visit those homes that you choose. Your Realtor will accompany you on these home visits and can usually map out the most effective route to see several properties in one day. They can recommend Open Houses for you to attend in your desired neighborhoods and provide information on homes recently sold in those areas. This is important information to have in negotiating prices when you decide on a home and want to make an offer.

It is important to have your Realtor or their associate with you in touring these homes. They may see problems or concerns with the home or the neighborhood that may not catch your attention. Remember, your Realtor is your advocate throughout the process of buying your home, and they take an oath and ethics courses to be sure you are treated lawfully and fairly throughout the transaction. You can call attention to details or concerns you may have about the home that your Realtor will be sure are addressed during a home inspection, if you choose to make an offer. Hopefully, your search will be short and your decision comes quickly!

Notes:

Is This

A Good Price

For This

Home?

7 PRICE COMPARISONS

Sellers use recently sold prices to determine their asking price. With your Realtor and the most currently sold properties in that neighborhood, you can use that analysis to determine fair market value. This will help you decide what to offer on a home. Many times sellers have that information, as well as an emotional attachment to the home that may increase the price they are asking. This is where your Realtor can really assist you in this negotiation. They can perform a Comparative Market Analysis (CMA) on the home and the previously sold or currently offered homes in the area. This data allows them to add or subtract dollar amounts depending on what the home offers. These variables may include lot size, square footage of the home, number of bedrooms and bathrooms, whether the interior is updated, private pool vs. community pool vs. no pool, outdoor kitchen, etc. They can then educate you on what a fair offer would be for the property, rather than the seller telling you the value of their home. Making an offer on the home is your decision and the offering price is also your decision.

Your Realtor can provide invaluable information in helping you arrive at that price, but this is your decision! So, consult with your Realtor to determine your offer. Be reasonable. Home buyers who are willing to make minor concessions may appear more desirable to the sellers. When making an offer, that offer should be contingent on a satisfactory home inspection. Inspections that reveal needed renovations can be used as leverage for the buyer at the closing table. Why is all of this information about inspections and making an offer in the chapter on price comparisons? Because once you start talking about the money part of the transaction and the safety of the property, you will quickly learn what you can and cannot live without in a home. This may cause you to go back and change your criteria that you originally started looking for in a home. Should you tell your Realtor or just change Realtors? By all means tell your Realtor! The better your Realtor knows you and your needs, the better they can serve you! This relationship with your Realtor is, hopefully, one that will last beyond one transaction. As we said in Chapter 5 - everyone's needs change depending on their stage in life. As you discuss the CMA on a property, let your Realtor know if you want to make an offer or change what type of home and amenities you want.

Notes:

_____

_____

_____

_____

_____

_____

_____

_____

_____

_____

This Home is Perfect!
I Love It!

8 INSPECTIONS

An inspection has nothing to do with the cosmetic aspects of the home, but everything to do with the safety of the home. It is a critical step in determining that the home is safe and will uncover any areas that may require renovating. Buyers pay for their inspection   As such, it can help you in negotiations with the seller, but hurt you in getting financing, as the lender may not allow you to finance as much as you planned and may require you to put more money down in order to purchase the home. This explains why you will see distressed properties for sale as only an "all cash" deal. The sellers know the property will not pass an inspection and the buyer will not be able to obtain financing.

But for your new dream home, what is involved in an inspection?

First and foremost, your Realtor will be onsite for the inspection. Remember, they are your advocate and they want to be sure nothing is missed in reviewing the safety of the home, and may want to call attention to problems you identified on your home visit.

What will be inspected?

A home inspection is an objective visual examination of the physical structure of a house, from the roof to the foundation.

The standard home inspector's report will cover the condition of the home's heating and air conditioning system; interior plumbing and electrical systems; walls ceilings, floors, windows, and doors; the roof, attic, and visible insulation; the foundation, basement and structural components.

Buying a home could be the largest single investment you will ever make. To minimize surprises and unexpected difficulties, you want to learn as much as you can about a newly constructed or existing home before you buy it.

We have all seen the movie, "The Money Pit". While funny to watch, it would be wretched to experience.

A home inspection may identify the need for major repairs or builder oversights, and the need for maintenance to keep the home in good shape. After the inspection, you will know more about the house, which will allow you to make decisions with confidence.

The inspection will assure you that this property meets current building codes to safely occupy the home.

Notes:

_____

_____

_____

_____

_____

_____

_____

_____

_____

_____

_____

_____

_____

More

Money

Needed?

9 CLOSING COSTS

Closing costs vary by market, but generally are 1.5% - 4% of the purchase price. By law, prospective homebuyers are entitled to see them prior to closing date. Your Realtor can provide those for you early in the process. But what are closing costs?

As you own property, some responsibilities are paid concurrently as you make payments, such as your mortgage interest. Some fees are paid in arrears (at the end of the year), such as taxes. And some homeowner fees at paid in advance, such as financing fees. So at the closing, when the title to the property is transferred, the buyer may have to pay for financing, and the seller may have to pay the taxes owed thus far that year. There are title transfer fees to be paid, that may include state, county and municipal fees.

By law homebuyers are entitled to see an itemized list of fees required at closing no later that 3 days prior to the closing date.

At times you will see a home offered with the caveat:

"Seller will pay $XX towards closing costs". This is a bonus for buyers and does not mean there is anything wrong with the property- only that the seller is motivated to move.

Again, your Realtor can provide these numbers for you early in the process to assist you in preparing for the closing.

Notes:

_____

_____

_____

_____

_____

_____

_____

_____

_____

_____

_____

_____

Let's

Make

A

Deal!

here. Insert chapter nine text here. Insert chapter nine text here. Insert chapter nine text here. Insert chapter nine

10 MAKE AN OFFER

You have your inspection results and all looks good. Time to make an offer! Consult with your Realtor to determine a reasonable offer. Be ready to negotiate! Be reasonable! You have your Comparative Market Analysis (CMA) as a guide. Other factors to consider are length of time the property has been on the market; how motivated is the seller; and a number of other variables. The seller has one property to sell, you have funds to take anywhere. You and your Realtor can make it happen! You found your dream home, now make it yours!

Notes:

_____

_____

_____

_____

_____

_____

_____

_____

_____

_____

_____

_____

ABOUT THE AUTHOR

After 30 years as a nurse, one of the most trusted professions in the country, Greta Nelson became a Realtor in Southwest Florida. Just as in nursing, her ethics drive her to provide the best service to her clients. Whether, buying, selling or investing, her clients' best interests are of primary importance. Reach out with questions: ggmnelson@aol.com